The Pattern Library

TPL™

Volume Two • I - Z

Little Acorn Books™

The Pattern Library

I-Z

• instruments • tools • pets • wild, exotic & domestic animals • maps • transportation • food • containers • vegetables •
• inventions • appliances • household objects • architecture • dinosaurs • plants • insects • sea creatures • and more.

by Marilynn G. Barr

LAB201412P
THE PATTERN LIBRARY • VOLUME TWO • I - Z

black and white, large illustrations in printable pattern format for:
• instruments • tools • pets • wild, exotic & domestic animals • maps • transportation • food • containers • vegetables •
• inventions • appliances • household objects • architecture • dinosaurs • plants • insects • sea creatures • and more. •

by Marilynn G. Barr

Published by: Little Acorn Books™
Originally published by: Monday Morning Books, Inc.

Little Acorn Books
PO Box 8787
Greensboro, NC 27419-0787

Promoting Early Skills for a Lifetime™

Little Acorn Books™
is an imprint of Little Acorn Associates, Inc.

http://www.littleacornbooks.com

ISBN 978-1-937257-63-7

Printed in the United States of America

The Pattern Library

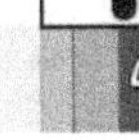

Table of Contents

Table of Contents

The Pattern Library

Volume Two • I - Z

Table of Contents

Table of Contents

More patterns for letters A through H are featured in *The Pattern Library™ • Volume One*, LAB201411P.

The Pattern Libary™ — is a two-volume treasury of large, black line illustrations in printable, pattern formats. This, **Volume Two** contains patterns for letters **I** through **Z**. It's a rich collection of illustrations from our image libraries and an invaluable resource for children, parents, teachers, crafters and anyone who requires blackline images for an infinite number or projects. Illustrations are labeled and easy-to-find as they appear alphabetically in the table of contents (pp. 3-6). Multiple versions of a given object or animal are also labeled accordingly in the table of contents.

Note: In most instances, patterns are listed by category or species names first with details, if any, in parenthesis:

lollipop (flat) - Volume 2, I-Z
lollipop (round) - Volume 2, I-Z
mouse (animated, winter) - Volume 2, I-Z
turtle (loggerhead) - Volume 2, I-Z

Patterns include a wide selection of items found around the house, around town, in recreational environments, domestic, wild, and exotic animals, musical instruments, tools, dwellings, containers, the vintage and the unique.

Decorate workstations, display and bulletin boards, take-home communications, work folders, book reports, book covers, scrapbooks, picture albums, stationary, desks, doors, windows, flags, paper bag lanterns, and daisy chains or embelish presentations.

Create activity sheets, picture word walls, flash cards, picture dictionaries, index fact cards, collages, matching card games, door knob hangers, signs, tags, labels, picture blocks, bag puppets, stick puppets, mobiles, flannel boards, and anything else you can imagine.

ibex

Maps are representations and boundaries are not exact.

ice cream (one scoop)

ice cream (five scoops)

ice (cube)

iceskate (left)

ice skate (right)

ice skate (left, with pompom)

ice skate (right, with pompom)

Idaho, USA

Maps are representations and boundaries are not exact.

igloo

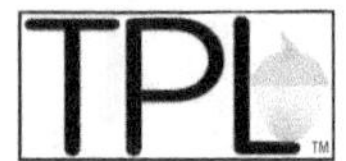

Illinois, USA

Maps are representations and boundaries are not exact.

Indiana, USA

Maps are representations and boundaries are not exact.

indri

ink (jar)

Iowa, USA

iron

ivy (outline)

LAB201412P • THE PATTERN LIBRARY • VOLUME TWO • I-Z • 978-1-937257-63-7 • © 2014 Little Acorn Books™

jack

jacks

jack o' lantern

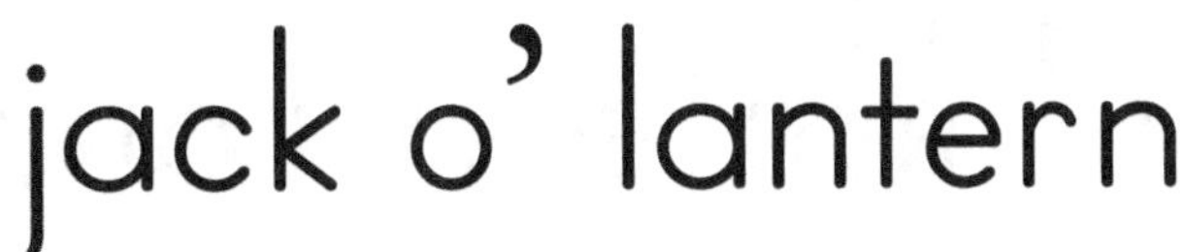

jack o' lantern (outline)

jack o' lantern (standard) 

jack rabbit

jack-in-the-box

jar

jellybeans

jellyfish

jonquil

 LAB201412P • THE PATTERN LIBRARY • VOLUME TWO • I-Z • 978-1-937257-63-7 • © 2014 Little Acorn Books™

jump rope

jumper

LAB201412P • THE PATTERN LIBRARY • VOLUME TWO • I-Z • 978-1-937257-63-7 • © 2014 Little Acorn Books™

kangaroo (animated)

kangaroo (outline)

LAB201412P • THE PATTERN LIBRARY • VOLUME TWO • I-Z • 978-1-937257-63-7 • © 2014 Little Acorn Books™

kangaroo (stylized)

Kansas, USA

Maps are representations and boundaries are not exact.

Kentucky, USA

Maps are representations and boundaries are not exact.

kerchief

kerchief

kettle

king

kinkajou

kite (box)

kite (standard)

kitten

knives (butter and steak)

koala

ladle (gravy)

LAB201412P • THE PATTERN LIBRARY • VOLUME TWO • I-Z • 978-1-937257-63-7 • © 2014 Little Acorn Books™

ladle (soup)

ladybug

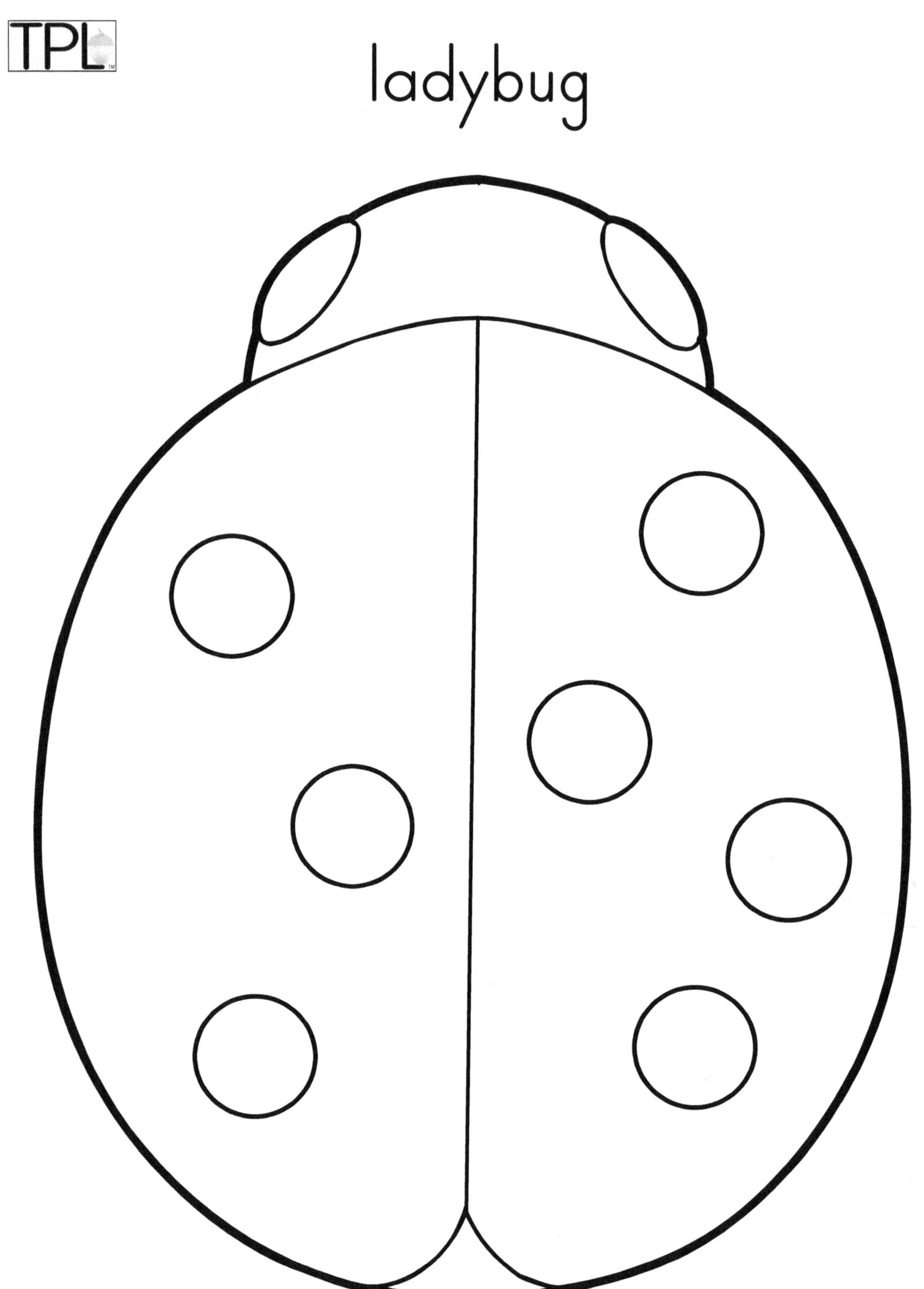

lamb

leaf (dogwood)

leaf (ginkgo)

leaf (hickory)

LAB201412P • THE PATTERN LIBRARY • VOLUME TWO • I-Z • 978-1-937257-63-7 • © 2014 Little Acorn Books™

leaf (maple)

leaf (maple, outline)

LAB201412P • THE PATTERN LIBRARY • VOLUME TWO • I-Z • 978-1-937257-63-7 • © 2014 Little Acorn Books™

leaf (oak)

leopard

leprechaun

leprechaun (torso)

light bulb

lion (head)

LAB201412P • THE PATTERN LIBRARY • VOLUME TWO • I-Z • 978-1-937257-63-7 • © 2014 Little Acorn Books™

lion (laying)

lizard

LAB201412P • THE PATTERN LIBRARY • VOLUME TWO • I-Z • 978-1-937257-63-7 • © 2014 Little Acorn Books™

llama

lobster

lock

lollipop (flat)

lollipop (round)

Louisiana, USA

Maps are representations and boundaries are not exact.

Louisiana Purchase

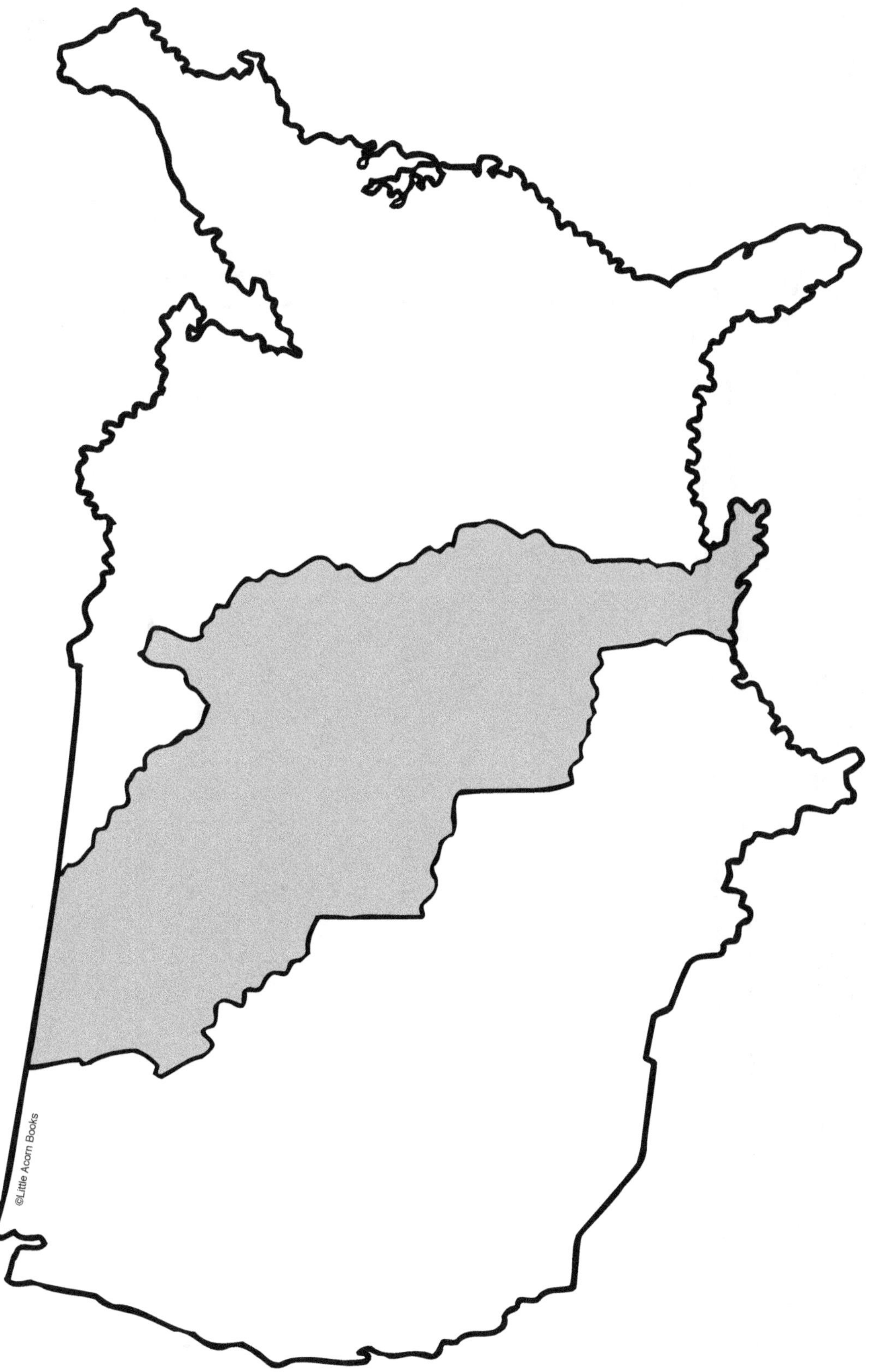

Maps are representations and boundaries are not exact.

lunch box

lyre

Maine, USA

Maps are representations and boundaries are not exact.

manatee

mandolin

madril

Manitoba, Canada

Maps are representations and boundaries are not exact.

maracas

Maryland, USA

Maps are representations and boundaries are not exact.

mask (tiger)

masks

LAB201412P • THE PATTERN LIBRARY • VOLUME TWO • I-Z • 978-1-937257-63-7 • © 2014 Little Acorn Books™

Massachusetts, USA

Maps are representations and boundaries are not exact.

matches (closed book)

matches (open book)

menorah

 LAB201412P • THE PATTERN LIBRARY • VOLUME TWO • I-Z • 978-1-937257-63-7 • © 2014 Little Acorn Books™

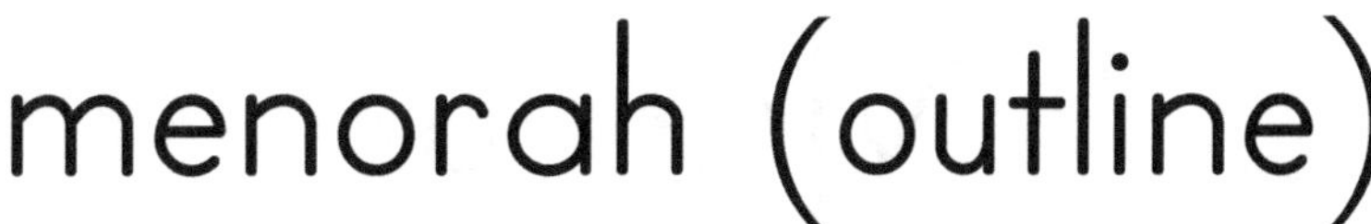
menorah (outline)

TPL

Mexico

Maps are representations and boundaries are not exact.

 LAB201412P • THE PATTERN LIBRARY • VOLUME TWO • I-Z • 978-1-937257-63-7 • © 2014 Little Acorn Books™

Michigan, USA

microscope

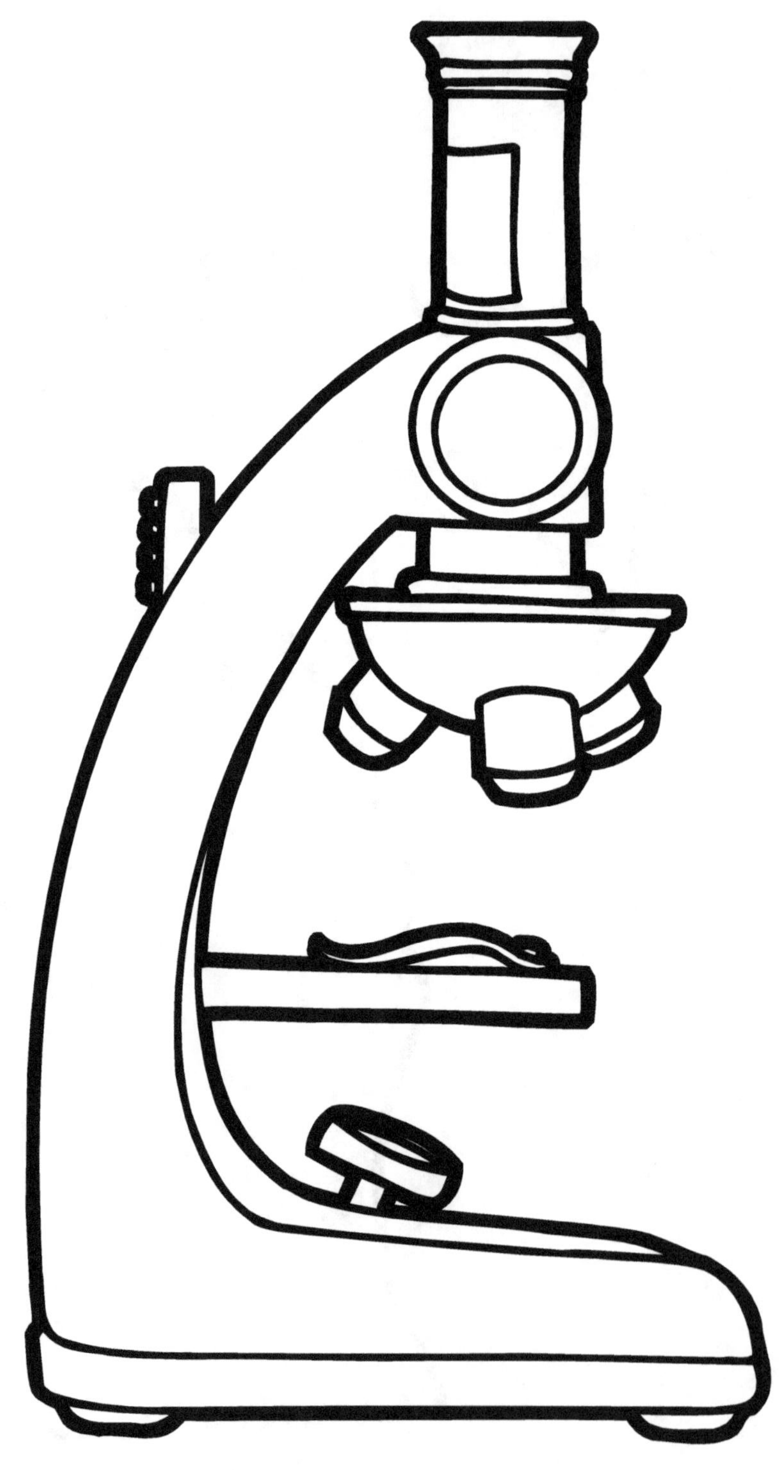

Minnesota, USA

Mississippi, USA

Maps are representations and boundaries are not exact.

Missouri, USA

Maps are representations and boundaries are not exact.

mitt (3D)

mitt (plain)

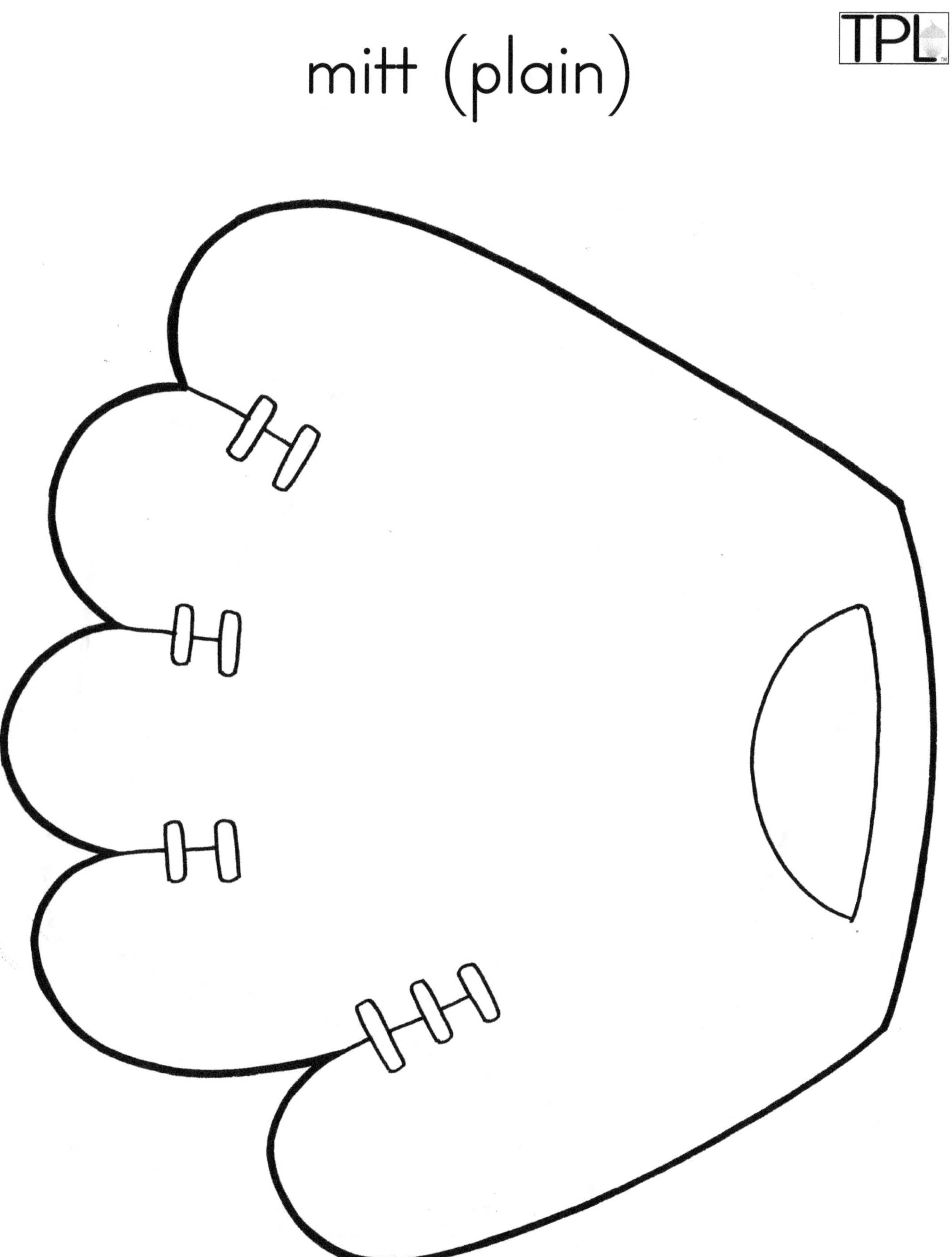

mitten (left)

mitten (right)

mittens

monkey

monster (head)

 LAB201412P • THE PATTERN LIBRARY • VOLUME TWO • I-Z • 978-1-937257-63-7 • © 2014 Little Acorn Books™

Montana, USA

Maps are representations and boundaries are not exact.

moon

LAB201412P • THE PATTERN LIBRARY • VOLUME TWO • I-Z • 978-1-937257-63-7 • © 2014 Little Acorn Books™

moon (with night cap)

moose

mouse (animated)

mouse (animated, waving)

 LAB201412P • THE PATTERN LIBRARY • VOLUME TWO • I-Z • 978-1-937257-63-7 • © 2014 Little Acorn Books™

mouse (animated, winter)

mushroom (bell-shaped)

mushroom (conical)

mushroom (convex)

LAB201412P • THE PATTERN LIBRARY • VOLUME TWO • I-Z • 978-1-937257-63-7 • © 2014 Little Acorn Books™

mushroom

(convex with skirt)

TPL™

narwhal

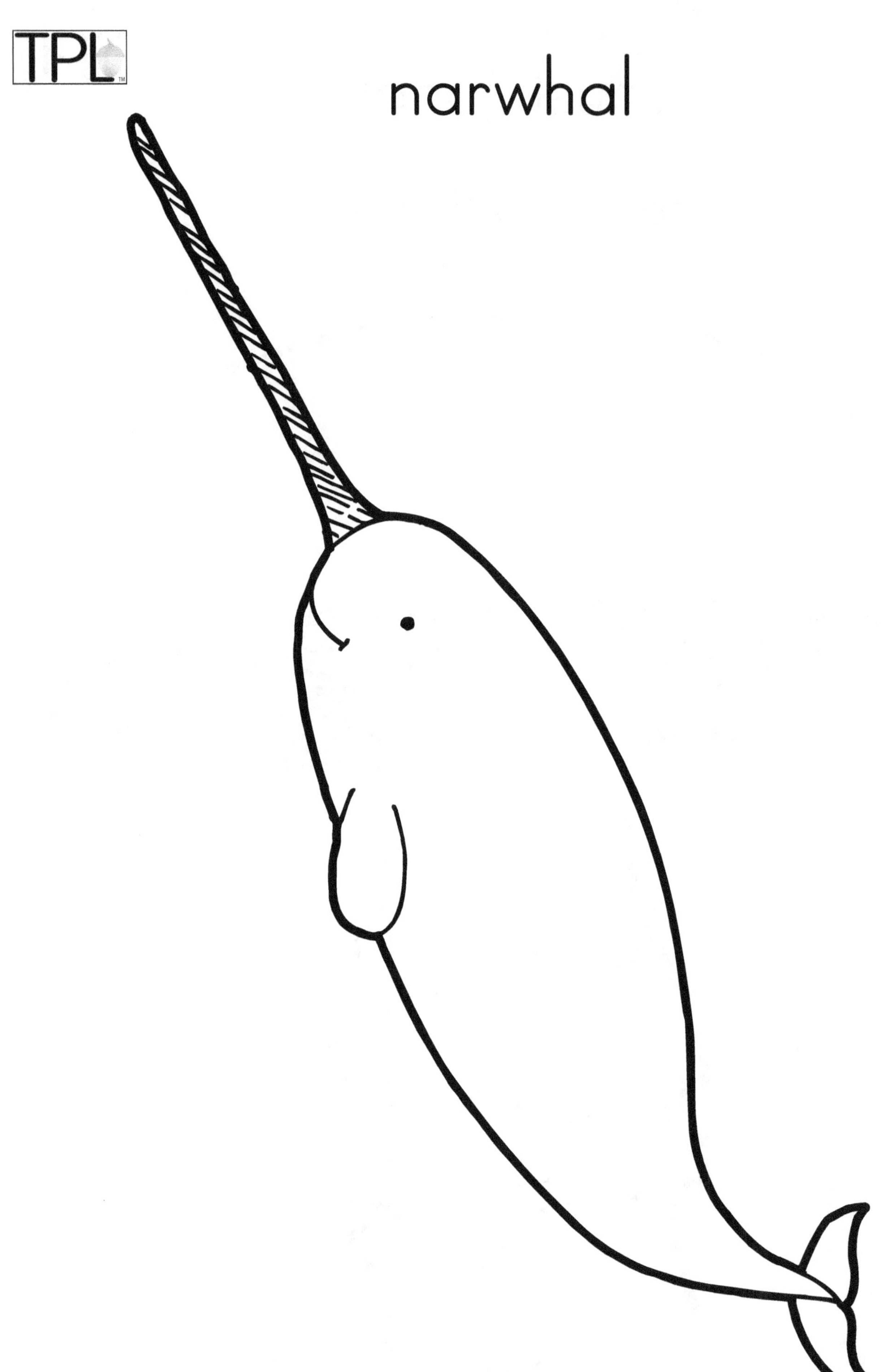

 LAB201412P • THE PATTERN LIBRARY • VOLUME TWO • I-Z • 978-1-937257-63-7 • © 2014 Little Acorn Books™

nautilus

Nebraska, USA

Maps are representations and boundaries are not exact.

necklace

necktie

needle (sewing)

nest

nest (outline)

net (without handle)

Nevada, USA

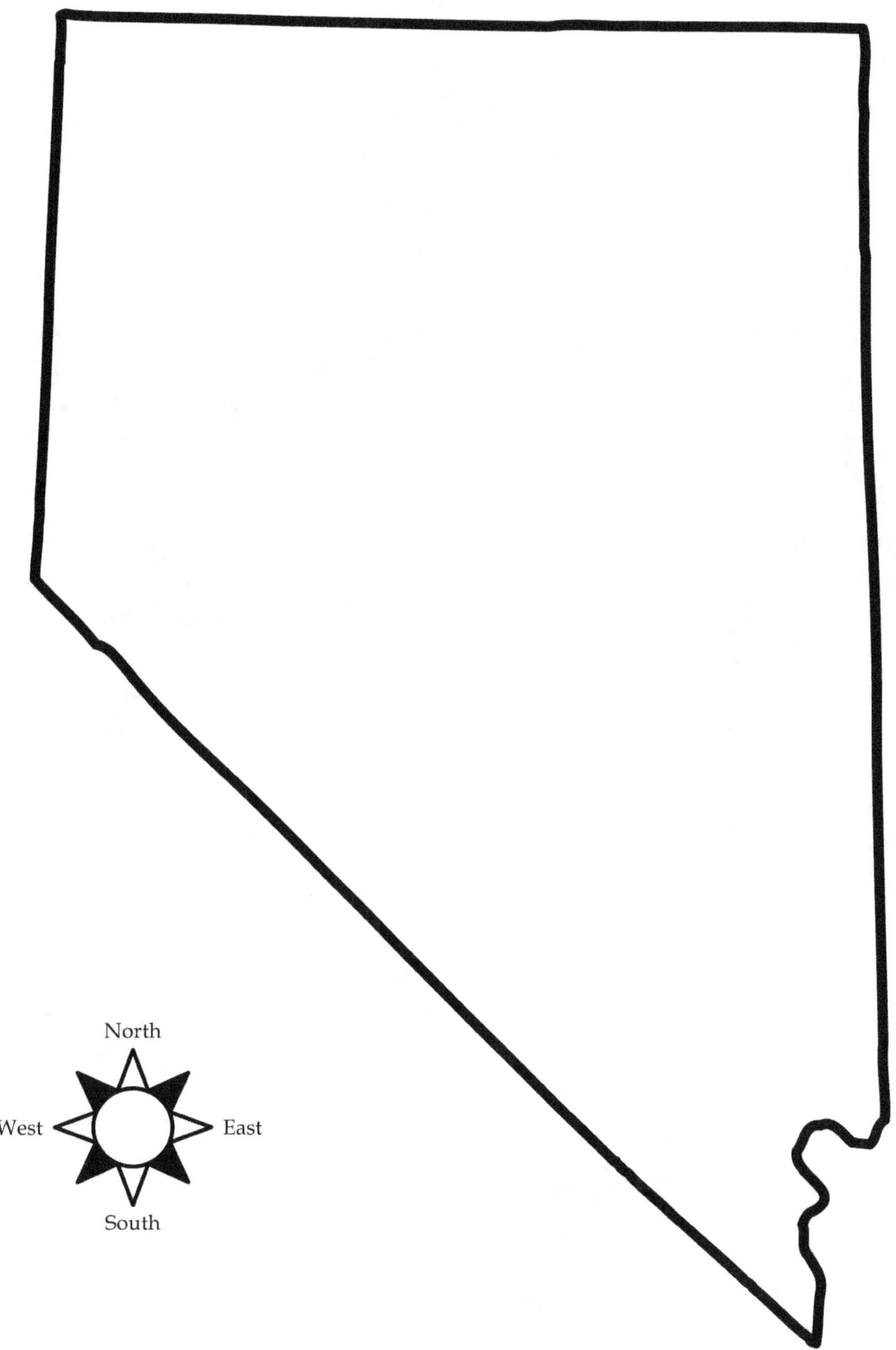

Maps are representations and boundaries are not exact.

New Brunswick, Canada

Maps are representations and boundaries are not exact.

Newfoundland & Labrador, Canada

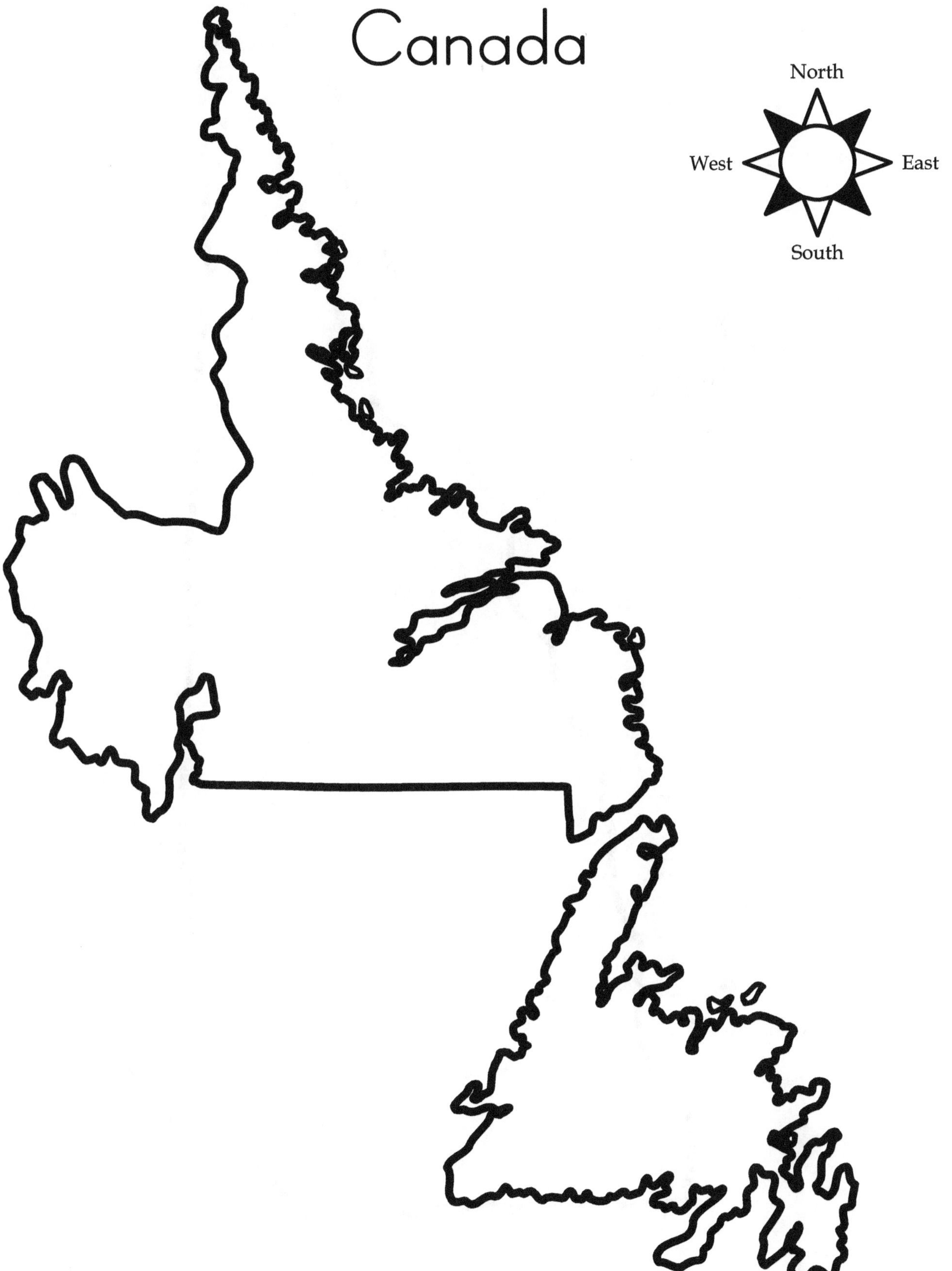

Maps are representations and boundaries are not exact.

New Hampshire, USA

Maps are representations and boundaries are not exact.

New Jersey, USA

Maps are representations and boundaries are not exact.

New Mexico, USA

Maps are representations and boundaries are not exact.

newspaper (folded)

New York, USA

Maps are representations and boundaries are not exact.

newt

nickels

North America

Maps are representations and boundaries are not exact.

North Carolina, USA

Maps are representations and boundaries are not exact.

North Dakota, USA

Maps are representations and boundaries are not exact.

Northern Territory &
Nunavut, Canada

Maps are representations and boundaries are not exact.

Nova Scotia, Canada

Maps are representations and boundaries are not exact.

octopus (floating)

 LAB201412P • THE PATTERN LIBRARY • VOLUME TWO • I-Z • 978-1-937257-63-7 • © 2014 Little Acorn Books™

octopus (poster)

octopus (sitting)

LAB201412P • THE PATTERN LIBRARY • VOLUME TWO • I-Z • 978-1-937257-63-7 • © 2014 Little Acorn Books™

Ohio, USA

okapi

Oklahoma, USA

Maps are representations and boundaries are not exact.

onion (spring)

 LAB201412P • THE PATTERN LIBRARY • VOLUME TWO • I-Z • 978-1-937257-63-7 • © 2014 Little Acorn Books™

Ontario, Canada

Maps are representations and boundaries are not exact.

orangutan

LAB201412P • THE PATTERN LIBRARY • VOLUME TWO • I-Z • 978-1-937257-63-7 • © 2014 Little Acorn Books™

Oregon, USA

Maps are representations and boundaries are not exact.

ornament (pear-shape)

ornament (round)

ostrich

LAB201412P • THE PATTERN LIBRARY • VOLUME TWO • I-Z • 978-1-937257-63-7 • © 2014 Little Acorn Books™

otter

overalls

owl

owl

ox (musk)

 LAB201412P • THE PATTERN LIBRARY • VOLUME TWO • I-Z • 978-1-937257-63-7 • © 2014 Little Acorn Books™

pail (handle down)

pail (handle up)

paintbrush (plain)

paintbrush (wide)

LAB201412P • THE PATTERN LIBRARY • VOLUME TWO • I-Z • 978-1-937257-63-7 • © 2014 Little Acorn Books™

paintbrushes (art)

palette (outline)

palette (outline)

palette (with paint daubs)

pan (frying)

papaya

paper plate

parachute

parrot

paste (jar)

paste (jar)

 LAB201412P • THE PATTERN LIBRARY • VOLUME TWO • I-Z • 978-1-937257-63-7 • © 2014 Little Acorn Books™

peanut

pear

 LAB201412P • THE PATTERN LIBRARY • VOLUME TWO • I-Z • 978-1-937257-63-7 • © 2014 Little Acorn Books™

peas

pens

LAB201412P • THE PATTERN LIBRARY • VOLUME TWO • I-Z • 978-1-937257-63-7 • © 2014 Little Acorn Books™

pencil (short and stout) 

pencil (standard)

LAB201412P • THE PATTERN LIBRARY • VOLUME TWO • I-Z • 978-1-937257-63-7 • © 2014 Little Acorn Books™

penguin

penguin (animated with hat)

 LAB201412P • THE PATTERN LIBRARY • VOLUME TWO • I-Z • 978-1-937257-63-7 • © 2014 Little Acorn Books™

pennies

Pennsylvania, USA

Maps are representations and boundaries are not exact.

pentagon (shape)

perch

pie

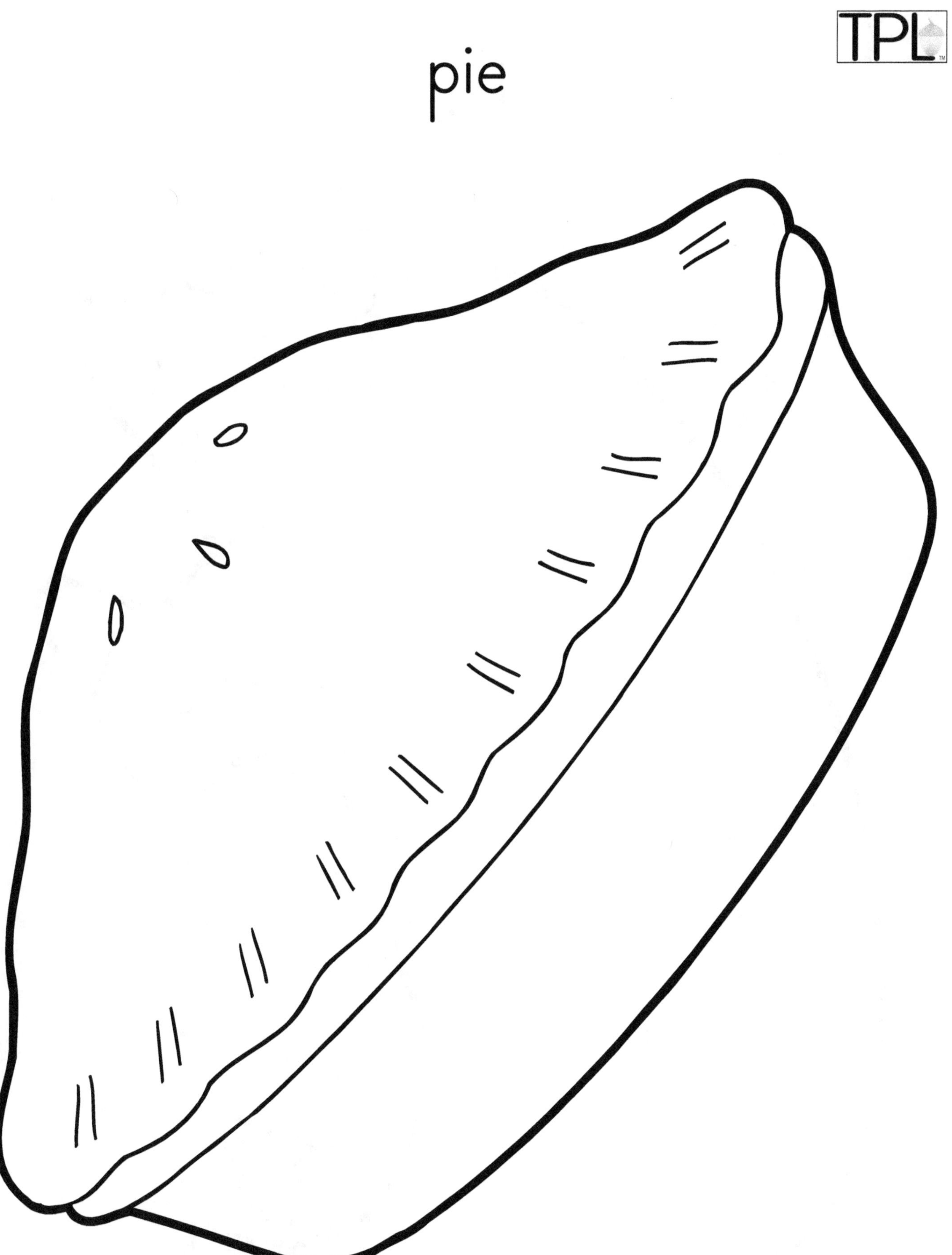

pig

pig (animated)

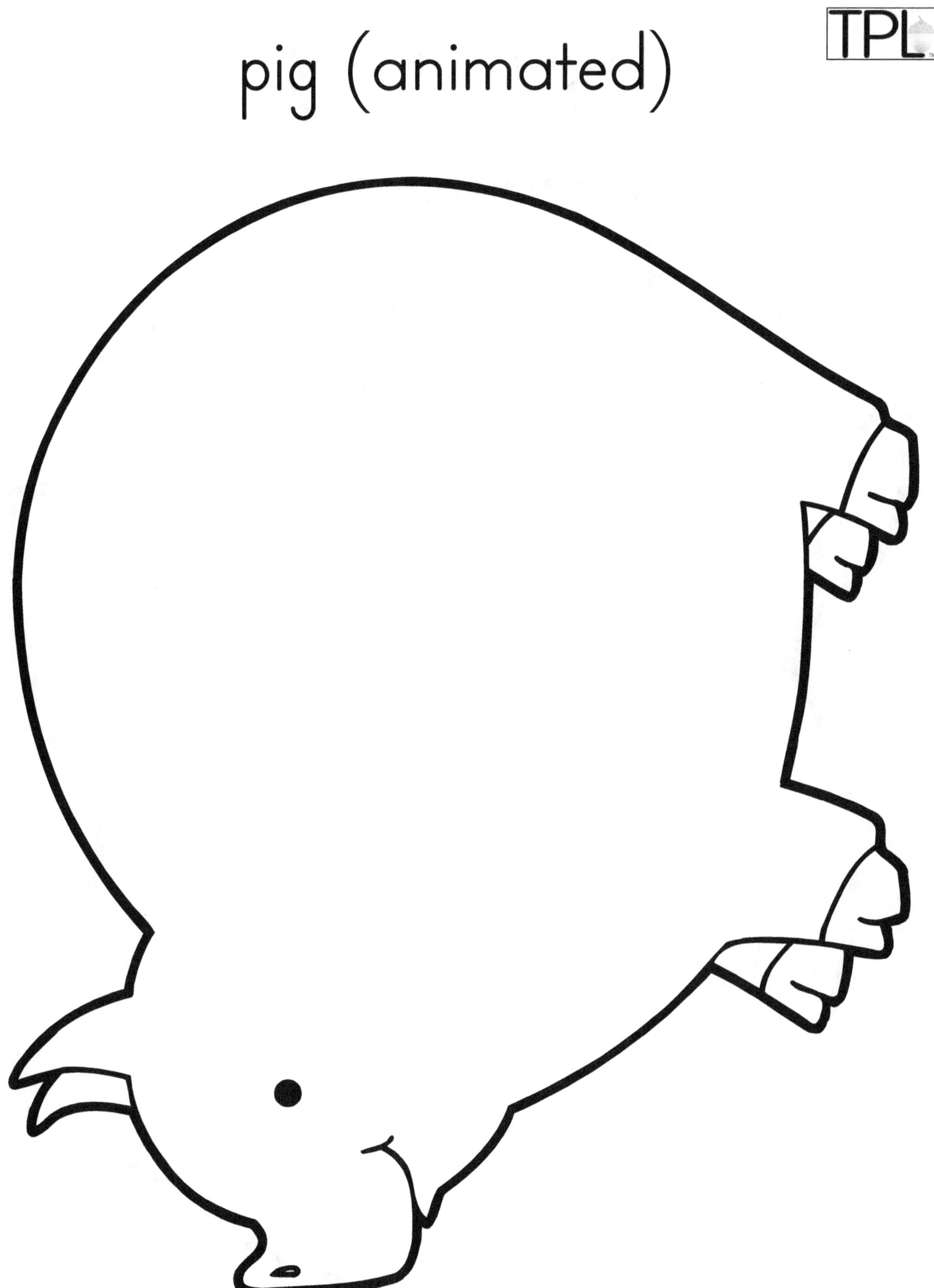

pig (outline)

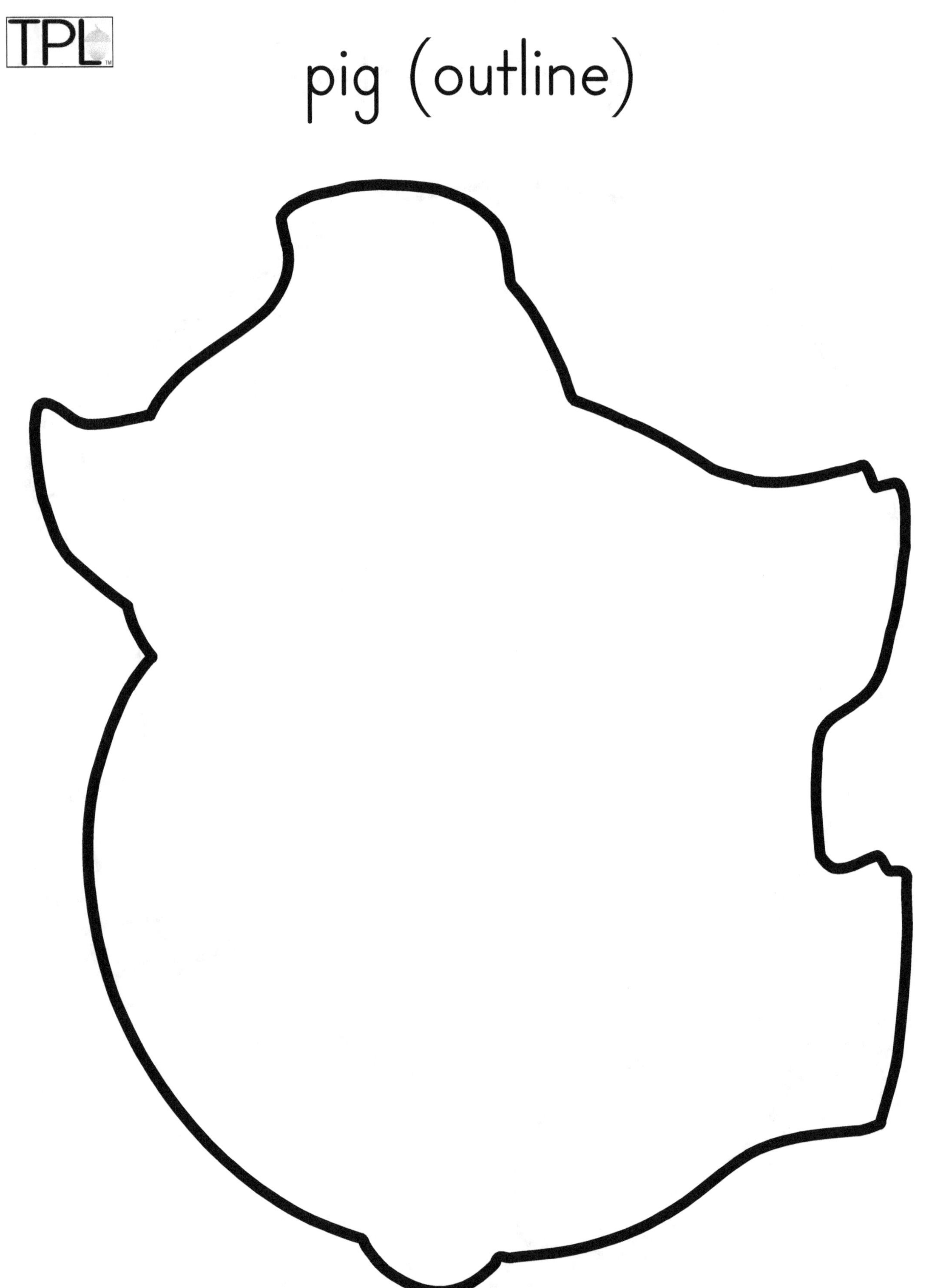

piggy bank

pinecone

LAB201412P • THE PATTERN LIBRARY • VOLUME TWO • I-Z • 978-1-937257-63-7 • © 2014 Little Acorn Books™

pink (crayon)

pitcher

planet (with ring)

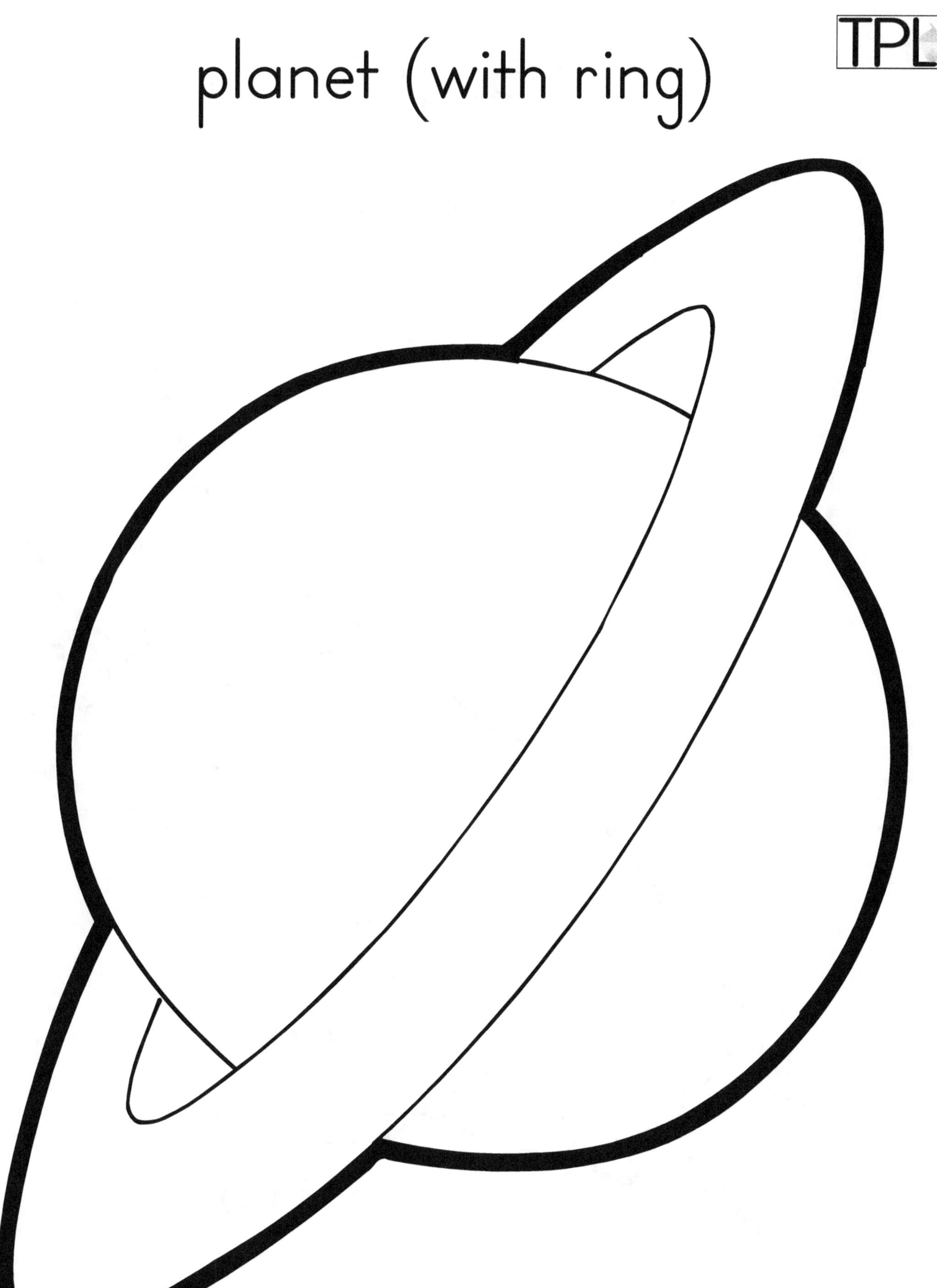

platypus

pocket (with stitches)

pocket watch

LAB201412P • THE PATTERN LIBRARY • VOLUME TWO • I-Z • 978-1-937257-63-7 • © 2014 Little Acorn Books™

poinsettia (with veins)

poinsettia (without veins)

pony

popsicle

LAB201412P • THE PATTERN LIBRARY • VOLUME TWO • I-Z • 978-1-937257-63-7 • © 2014 Little Acorn Books™

pot (cooking)

potato

LAB201412P • THE PATTERN LIBRARY • VOLUME TWO • I-Z • 978-1-937257-63-7 • © 2014 Little Acorn Books™

pretzel (twist)

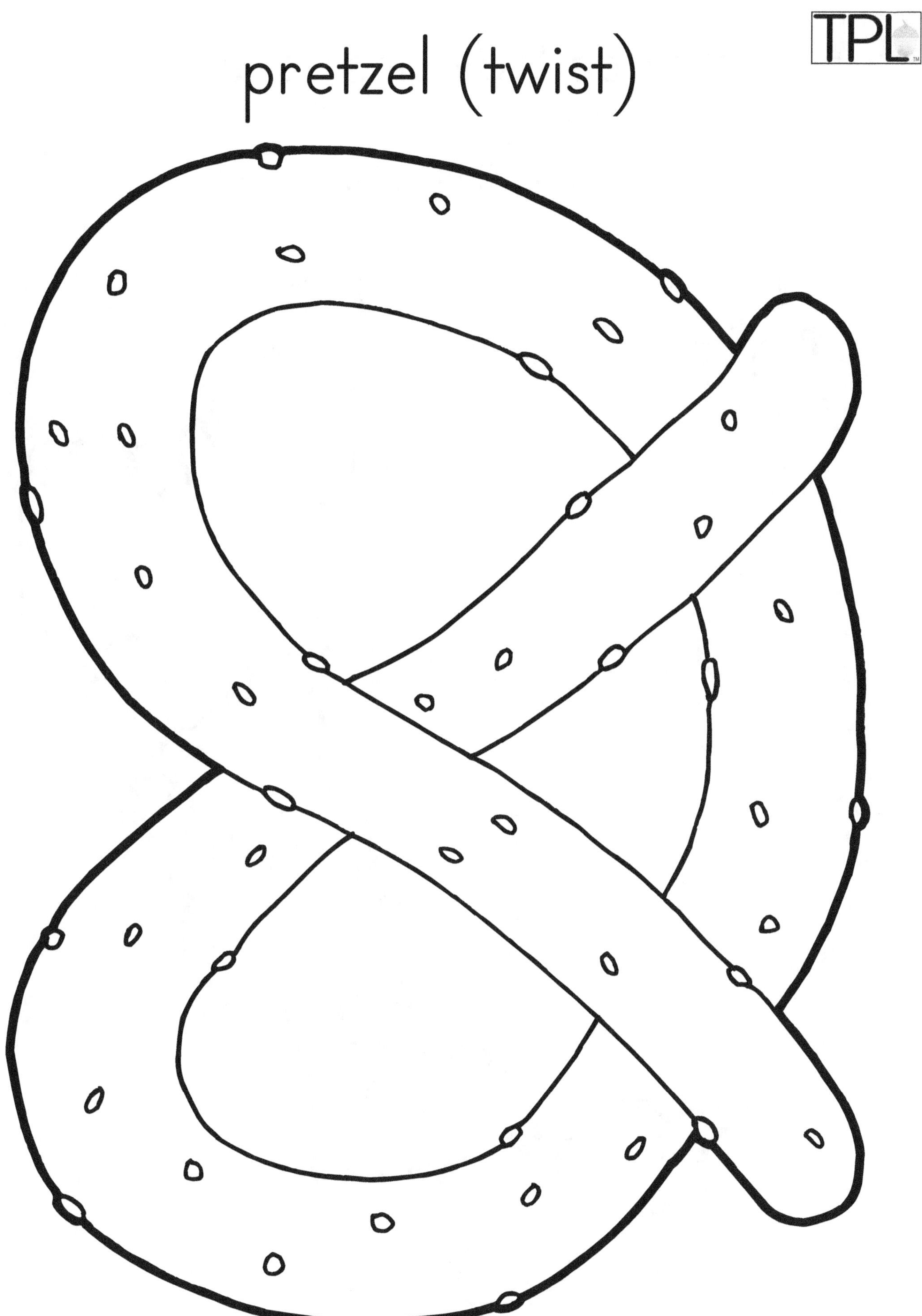

Prince Edward Island, Canada

Maps are representations and boundaries are not exact.

puffin

pumpkin

LAB201412P • THE PATTERN LIBRARY • VOLUME TWO • I-Z • 978-1-937257-63-7 • © 2014 Little Acorn Books™

pumpkin

pumpkin

puppy

purple (crayon)

LAB201412P • THE PATTERN LIBRARY • VOLUME TWO • I-Z • 978-1-937257-63-7 • © 2014 Little Acorn Books™

pushpin

pyramid

 LAB201412P • THE PATTERN LIBRARY • VOLUME TWO • I-Z • 978-1-937257-63-7 • © 2014 Little Acorn Books™

quail (animated)

quail (stylized)

quarters

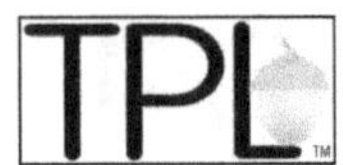

Quebec, Canada

Maps are representations and boundaries are not exact.

queen

question mark

LAB201412P • THE PATTERN LIBRARY • VOLUME TWO • I-Z • 978-1-937257-63-7 • © 2014 Little Acorn Books™

quetzal

quill (pen)

quilt

quiver

rabbit (animated, waving)

rabbit (animated, floppy ears)

LAB201412P • THE PATTERN LIBRARY • VOLUME TWO • I-Z • 978-1-937257-63-7 • © 2014 Little Acorn Books™

rabbit (chocolate)

rabbit (outline)

LAB201412P • THE PATTERN LIBRARY • VOLUME TWO • I-Z • 978-1-937257-63-7 • © 2014 Little Acorn Books™

rabbit (stylized)

raccoon

 LAB201412P • THE PATTERN LIBRARY • VOLUME TWO • I-Z • 978-1-937257-63-7 • © 2014 Little Acorn Books™

raccoon (waving)

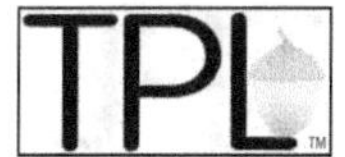

raindrop

ram

red (crayon)

reindeer

rhinoceros

LAB201412P • THE PATTERN LIBRARY • VOLUME TWO • I-Z • 978-1-937257-63-7 • © 2014 Little Acorn Books™

Rhode Island, USA

Maps are representations and boundaries are not exact.

rollerskate (left)

LAB201412P • THE PATTERN LIBRARY • VOLUME TWO • I-Z • 978-1-937257-63-7 • © 2014 Little Acorn Books™

rollerskate (right)

rollerskate (child, left)

rollerskate (child, right)

rooster (animated)

rooster (stylized)

rose

safety pin (closed)

safety pin (open)

sailboat(outline)

salmon (Chinook)

sand pail poster

Saskatchewan, Canada 

Maps are representations and boundaries are not exact.

satellite

scissors (closed)

scissors (open)

LAB201412P • THE PATTERN LIBRARY • VOLUME TWO • I-Z • 978-1-937257-63-7 • © 2014 Little Acorn Books™

scissors (tailor's)

screw (flathead)

screw (Phillips)

screwdriver (flathead)

screwdriver (Phillips head)

seal (animated)

seal (animated, wearing hat)

seashell

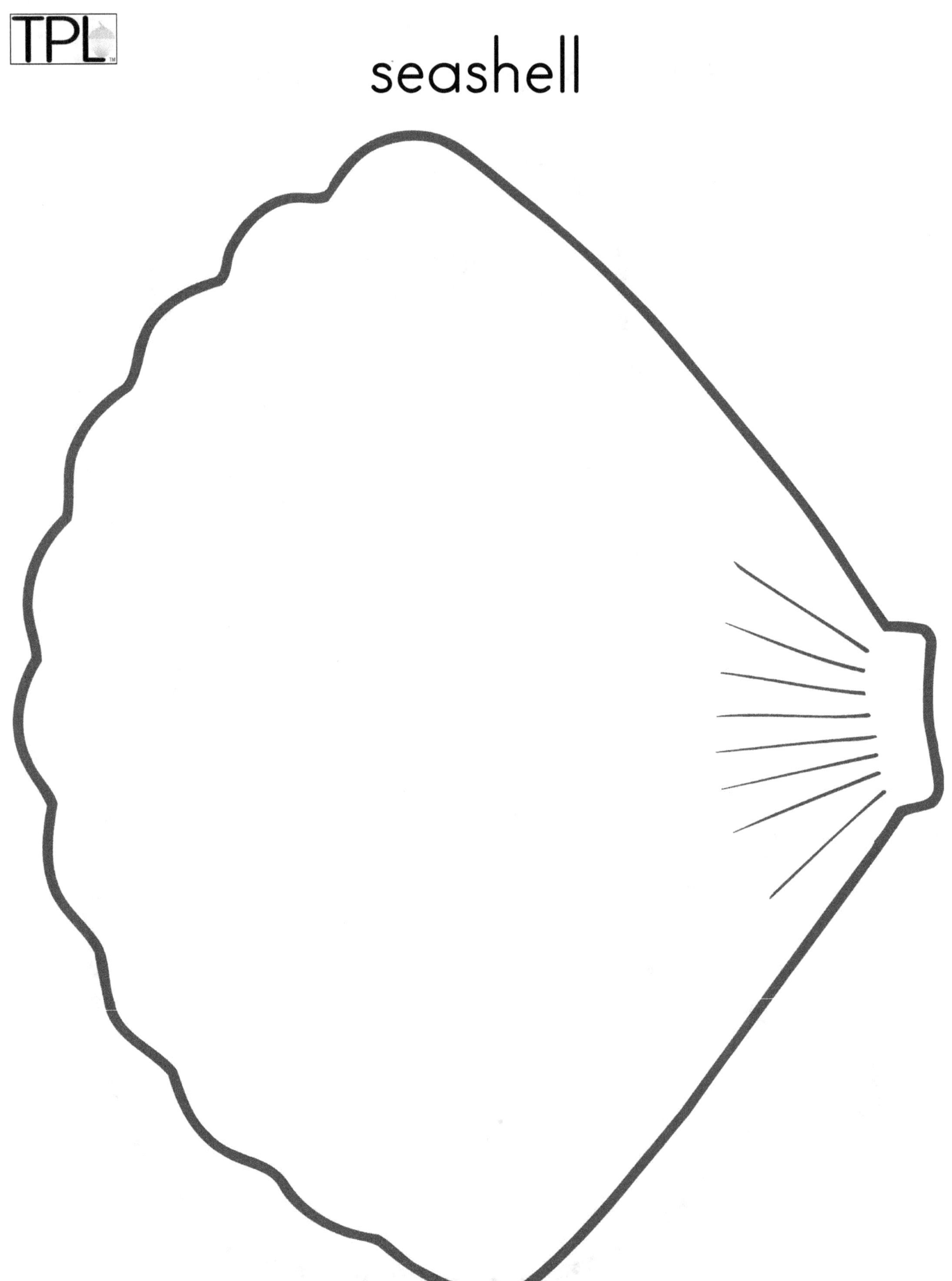

shaker (salt)

ship (toy)

shoe (left-buckle)

show (right-buckle)

shoe (left-loafer)

show (right-loafer)

 LAB201412P • THE PATTERN LIBRARY • VOLUME TWO • I-Z • 978-1-937257-63-7 • © 2014 Little Acorn Books™

shopping bag

shrew

silver (crayon)

LAB201412P • THE PATTERN LIBRARY • VOLUME TWO • I-Z • 978-1-937257-63-7 • © 2014 Little Acorn Books™

skeleton

skirt (pleated)

skunk

snail (animated)

snail (oultine)

snail (stylized)

snake

sneaker (left-high top)

sneaker (right-high top) TPL

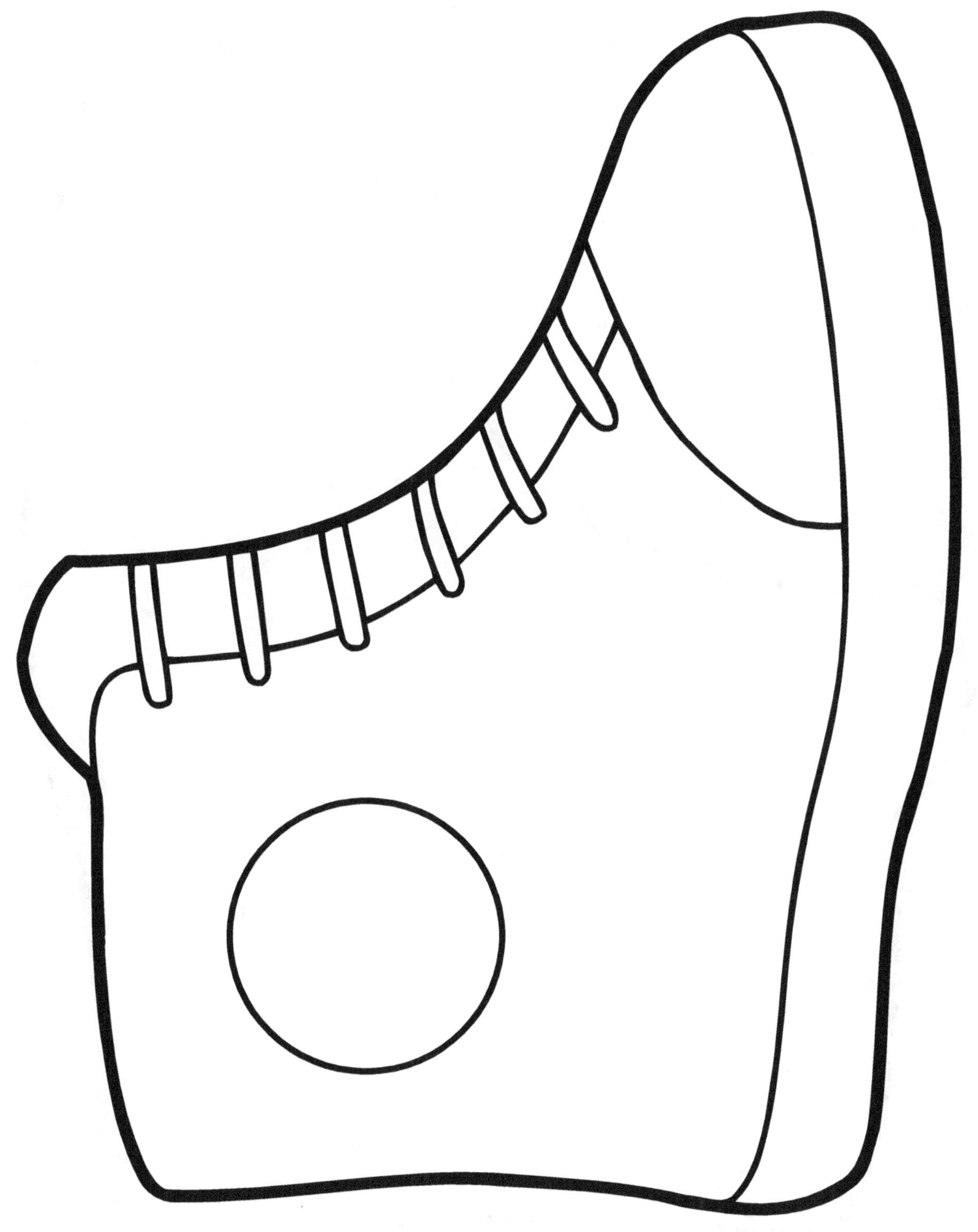

sneaker (outline-high top)

sneaker (outline-high top)

LAB201412P • THE PATTERN LIBRARY • VOLUME TWO • I-Z • 978-1-937257-63-7 • © 2014 Little Acorn Books™

snipe

snowflake

snowman

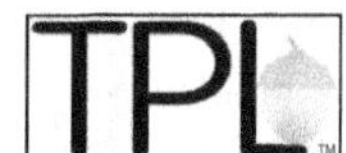

snowman (waving)

 LAB201412P • THE PATTERN LIBRARY • VOLUME TWO • I-Z • 978-1-937257-63-7 • © 2014 Little Acorn Books™

sock (left)

sock (right)

LAB201412P • THE PATTERN LIBRARY • VOLUME TWO • I-Z • 978-1-937257-63-7 • © 2014 Little Acorn Books™

sofa

sombrero

LAB201412P • THE PATTERN LIBRARY • VOLUME TWO • I-Z • 978-1-937257-63-7 • © 2014 Little Acorn Books™

South America

Maps are representations and boundaries are not exact.

South Carolina, USA

Maps are representations and boundaries are not exact.

South Dakota, USA

Maps are representations and boundaries are not exact.

 — TPL™ logo

space shuttle

space shuttle (in flight)

spade (symbol)

LAB201412P • THE PATTERN LIBRARY • VOLUME TWO • I-Z • 978-1-937257-63-7 • © 2014 Little Acorn Books™

spade (tool)

sphinx

spider

Spirit of St. Louis

spool

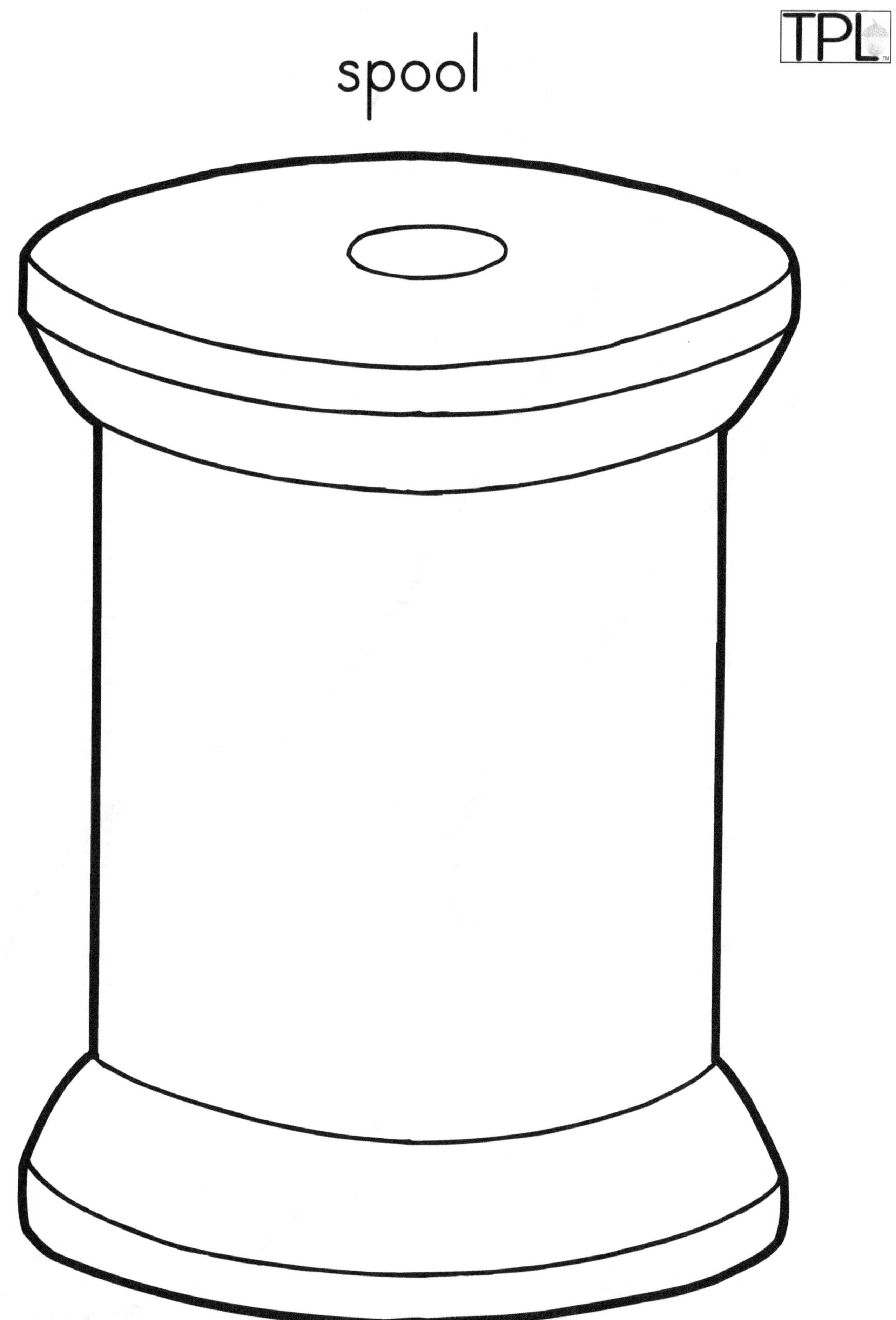

spoon (flat)

spoon

squirrel (animated)

squirrel (stylized)

squirrel (wearing sweater)

LAB201412P • THE PATTERN LIBRARY • VOLUME TWO • I-Z • 978-1-937257-63-7 • © 2014 Little Acorn Books™

stage

stagecoach

stapler

star (five points)

star (six points)

starfish

stocking (outline)

stomach

LAB201412P • THE PATTERN LIBRARY • VOLUME TWO • I-Z • 978-1-937257-63-7 • © 2014 Little Acorn Books™

strawberries

submarine (1898)

submarine

suitcase

 LAB201412P • THE PATTERN LIBRARY • VOLUME TWO • I-Z • 978-1-937257-63-7 • © 2014 Little Acorn Books™

sun (animated)

swan

tadpole

tamborine

LAB201412P • THE PATTERN LIBRARY • VOLUME TWO • I-Z • 978-1-937257-63-7 • © 2014 Little Acorn Books™

tan (crayon)

teacup

teacup and saucer

teapot

LAB201412P • THE PATTERN LIBRARY • VOLUME TWO • I-Z • 978-1-937257-63-7 • © 2014 Little Acorn Books™

telephone (1940s)

telephone (push buttons)

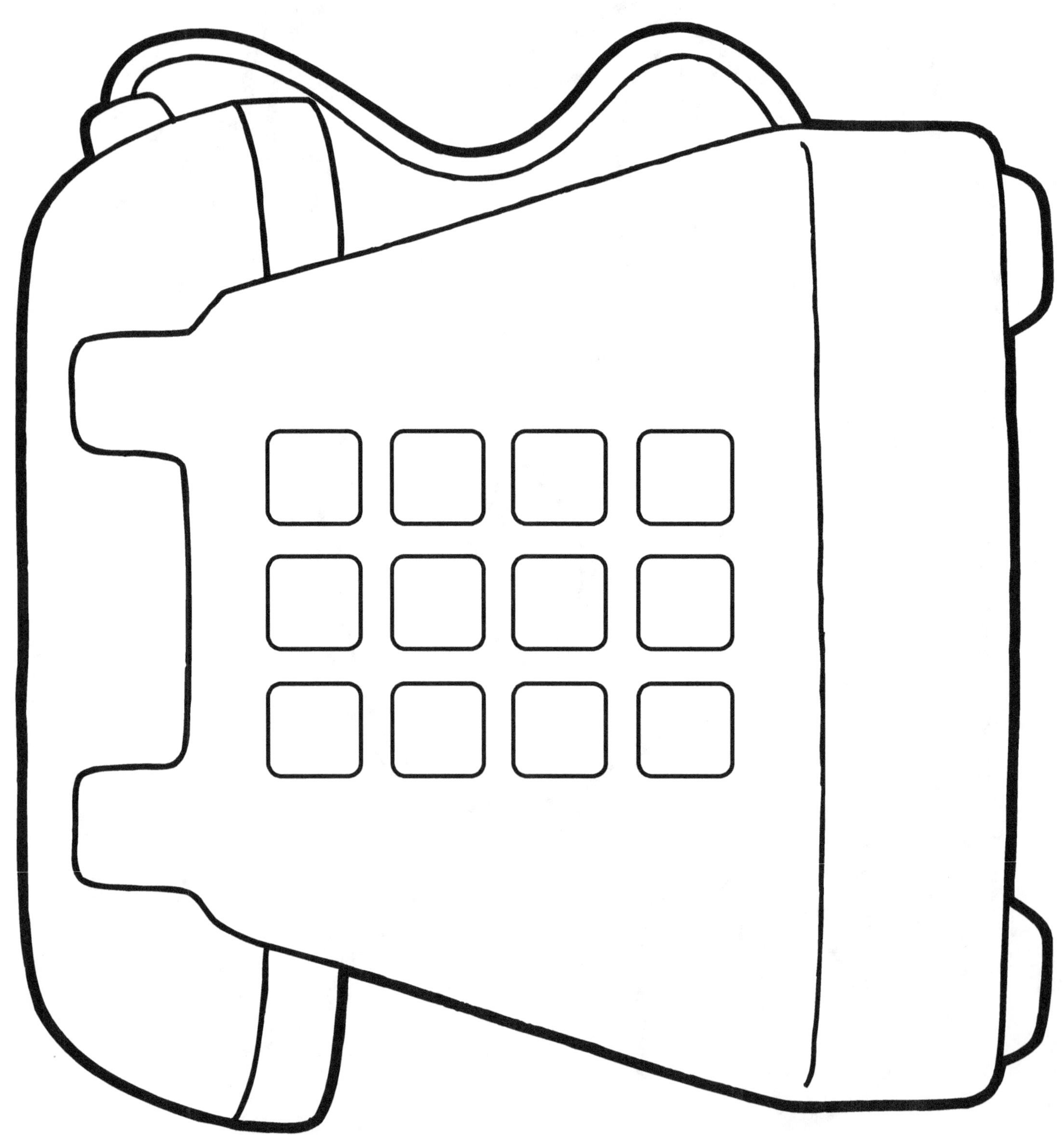

telephone (cordless)

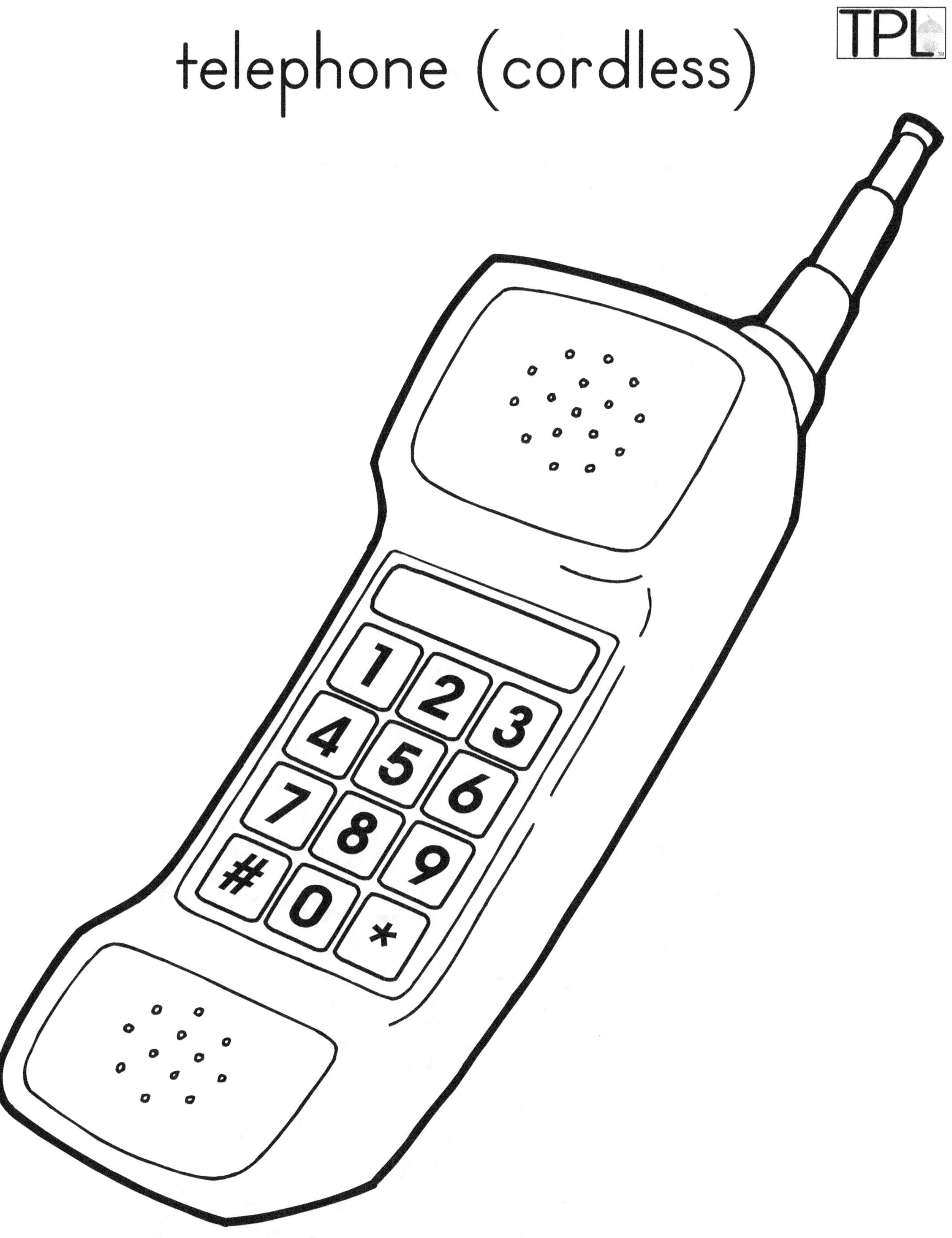

telephone (first)

LAB201412P • THE PATTERN LIBRARY • VOLUME TWO • I-Z • 978-1-937257-63-7 • © 2014 Little Acorn Books™

telephone (rotary dial)

telephone (slimline)

Tennessee, USA

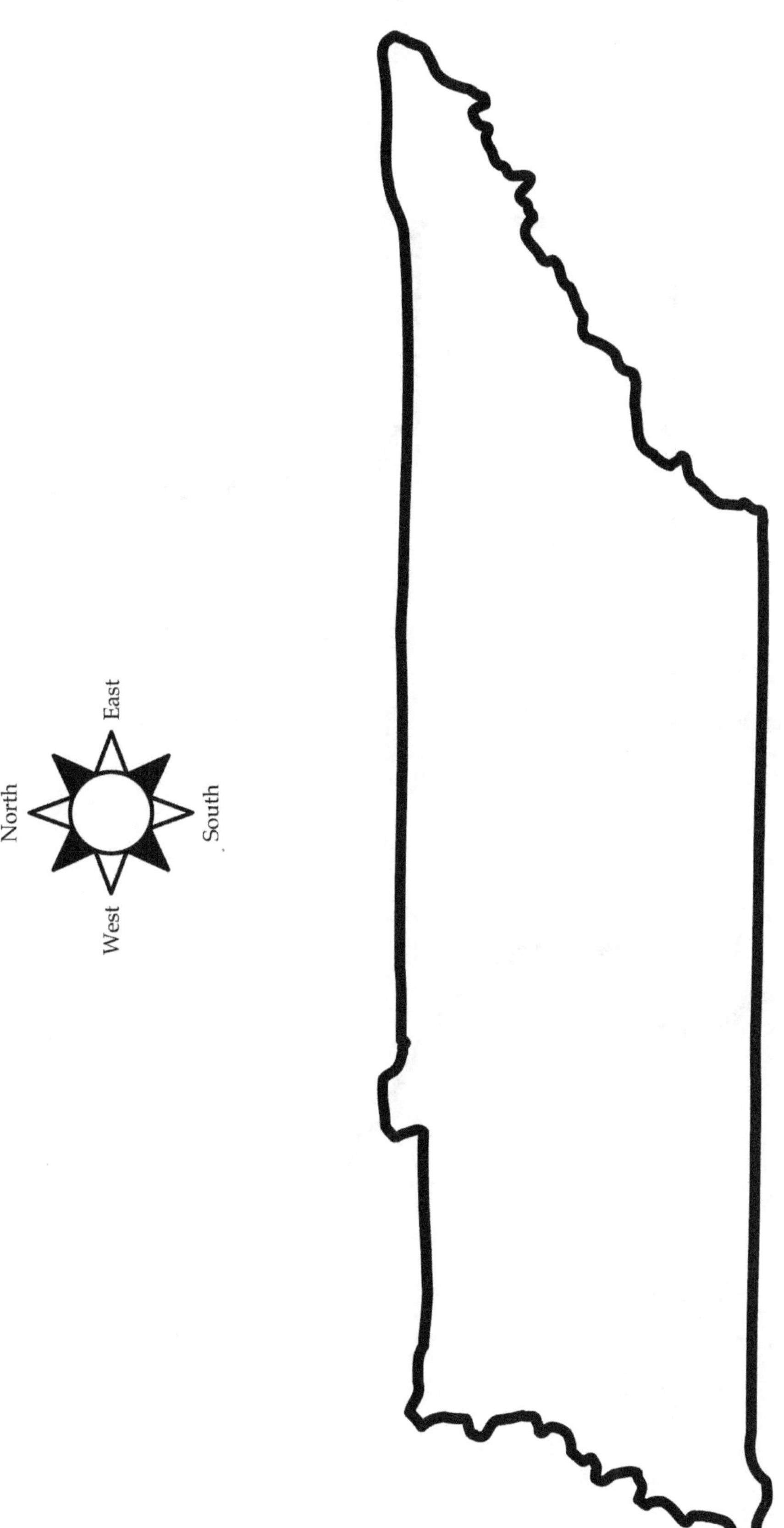

Texas, USA

Maps are representations and boundaries are not exact.

thimble

tiger

 LAB201412P • THE PATTERN LIBRARY • VOLUME TWO • I-Z • 978-1-937257-63-7 • © 2014 Little Acorn Books™

tire

tire

tomato

tooth

LAB201412P • THE PATTERN LIBRARY • VOLUME TWO • I-Z • 978-1-937257-63-7 • © 2014 Little Acorn Books™

tooth (molar)

toothbrush

LAB201412P • THE PATTERN LIBRARY • VOLUME TWO • I-Z • 978-1-937257-63-7 • © 2014 Little Acorn Books™

toothpaste

toucan

LAB201412P • THE PATTERN LIBRARY • VOLUME TWO • I-Z • 978-1-937257-63-7 • © 2014 Little Acorn Books™

toucan (outline)

tractor

LAB201412P • THE PATTERN LIBRARY • VOLUME TWO • I-Z • 978-1-937257-63-7 • © 2014 Little Acorn Books™

traffic signal

tree

tree (pine)

triangle

LAB201412P • THE PATTERN LIBRARY • VOLUME TWO • I-Z • 978-1-937257-63-7 • © 2014 Little Acorn Books™

tricycle

trowel

truck

trunk (storage)

 LAB201412P • THE PATTERN LIBRARY • VOLUME TWO • I-Z • 978-1-937257-63-7 • © 2014 Little Acorn Books™

trunk (tree)

tub

LAB201412P • THE PATTERN LIBRARY • VOLUME TWO • I-Z • 978-1-937257-63-7 • © 2014 Little Acorn Books™

tube (cardboard)

tulip

LAB201412P • THE PATTERN LIBRARY • VOLUME TWO • I-Z • 978-1-937257-63-7 • © 2014 Little Acorn Books™

tuna

tuna

turkey

LAB201412P • THE PATTERN LIBRARY • VOLUME TWO • I-Z • 978-1-937257-63-7 • © 2014 Little Acorn Books™

turkey (hen)

turkey (outline)

LAB201412P • THE PATTERN LIBRARY • VOLUME TWO • I-Z • 978-1-937257-63-7 • © 2014 Little Acorn Books™

turkey (tom)

tuquoise (crayon)

LAB201412P • THE PATTERN LIBRARY • VOLUME TWO • I-Z • 978-1-937257-63-7 • © 2014 Little Acorn Books™

turtle (animated)

turtle (animated with hat)

turtle (loggerhead)

turtle (outline)

LAB201412P • THE PATTERN LIBRARY • VOLUME TWO • I-Z • 978-1-937257-63-7 • © 2014 Little Acorn Books™

turtle (pet)

turtledove

typewriter (1867)

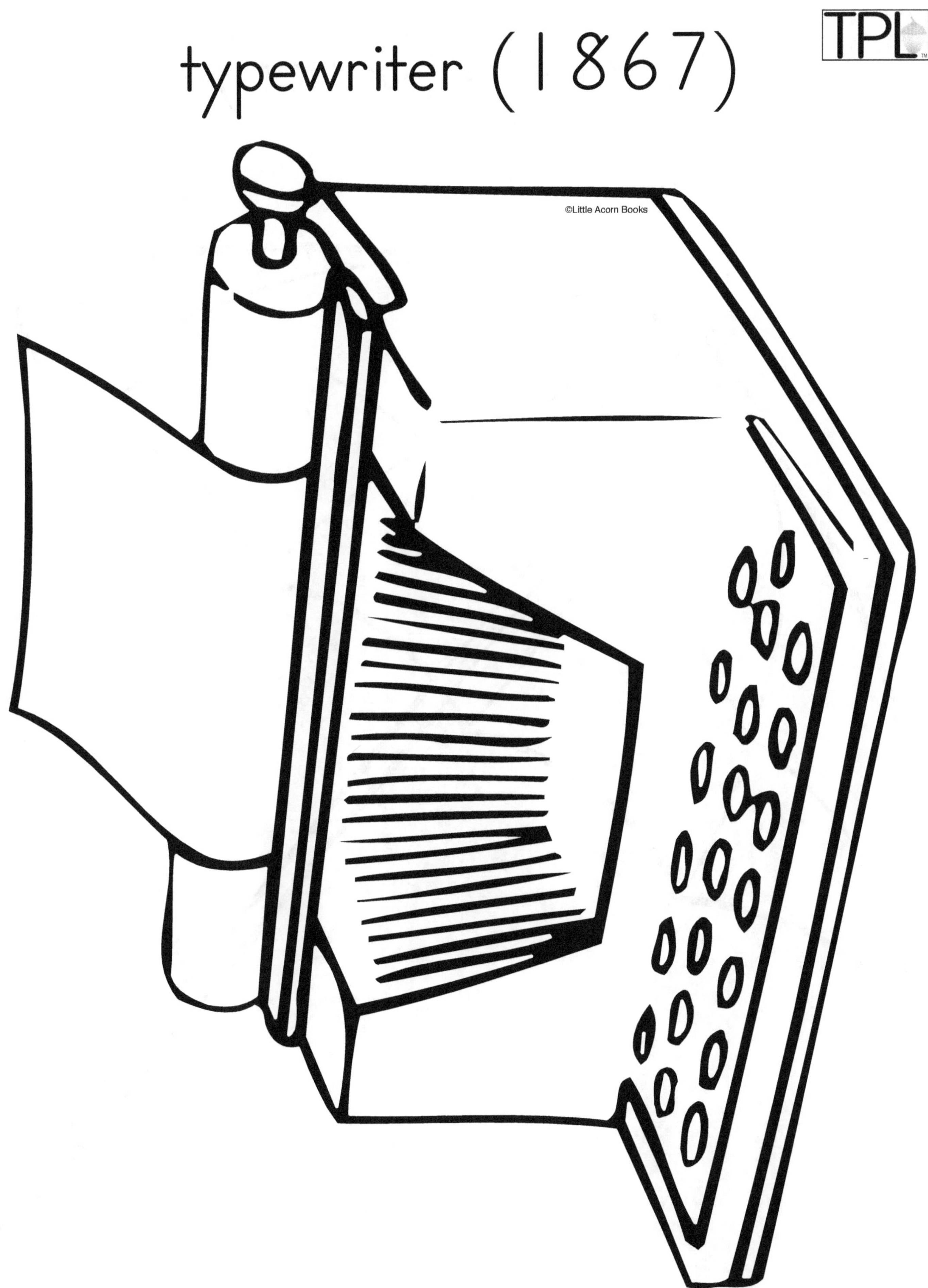

umbrella (beach)

LAB201412P • THE PATTERN LIBRARY • VOLUME TWO • I-Z • 978-1-937257-63-7 • © 2014 Little Acorn Books™

umbrella (outline)

umbrella (rain)

umpire

underwear

unicycle

unicycle

United Kingdom

Maps are representations and boundaries are not exact.

Maps are representations and boundaries are not exact.

USS Constitution

Utah, USA

Maps are representations and boundaries are not exact.

vacuum cleaner (1908)

vacuum cleaner (upright)

LAB201412P • THE PATTERN LIBRARY • VOLUME TWO • I-Z • 978-1-937257-63-7 • © 2014 Little Acorn Books™

Valentine candy box

van

vase

venus flytrap

LAB201412P • THE PATTERN LIBRARY • VOLUME TWO • I-Z • 978-1-937257-63-7 • © 2014 Little Acorn Books™

Vermont, USA

Maps are representations and boundaries are not exact.

LAB201412P • THE PATTERN LIBRARY • VOLUME TWO • I-Z • 978-1-937257-63-7 • © 2014 Little Acorn Books™

vicuña

viking

LAB201412P • THE PATTERN LIBRARY • VOLUME TWO • I-Z • 978-1-937257-63-7 • © 2014 Little Acorn Books™

violin

Virginia, USA

Maps are representations and boundaries are not exact.

visor

volcano

LAB201412P • THE PATTERN LIBRARY • VOLUME TWO • I-Z • 978-1-937257-63-7 • © 2014 Little Acorn Books™

vole

volley ball

vulture

wagon (covered)

wagon (toy)

walrus

LAB201412P • THE PATTERN LIBRARY • VOLUME TWO • I-Z • 978-1-937257-63-7 • © 2014 Little Acorn Books™

Washington, USA

Maps are representations and boundaries are not exact.

Washington, DC
(District of Columbia, USA)

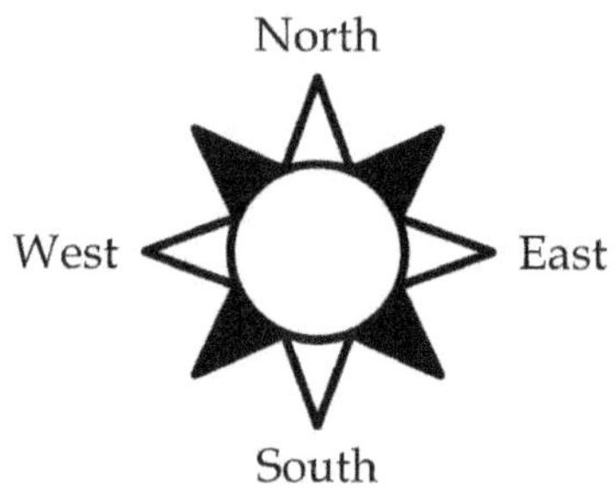

Maps are representations and boundaries are not exact.

watermelon (wedge)

watermelon (whole)

weasel

web (spider)

West Virginia, USA

Maps are representations and boundaries are not exact.

Western hemisphere

Maps are representations and boundaries are not exact.

whale (animated)

whale (humpback)

whale (outline)

wheel (spoked)

wheelbarrow

whip

 LAB201412P • THE PATTERN LIBRARY • VOLUME TWO • I-Z • 978-1-937257-63-7 • © 2014 Little Acorn Books™

whisk

whistle

   LAB201412P • THE PATTERN LIBRARY • VOLUME TWO • I-Z • 978-1-937257-63-7 • © 2014 Little Acorn Books™

White House, The, USA

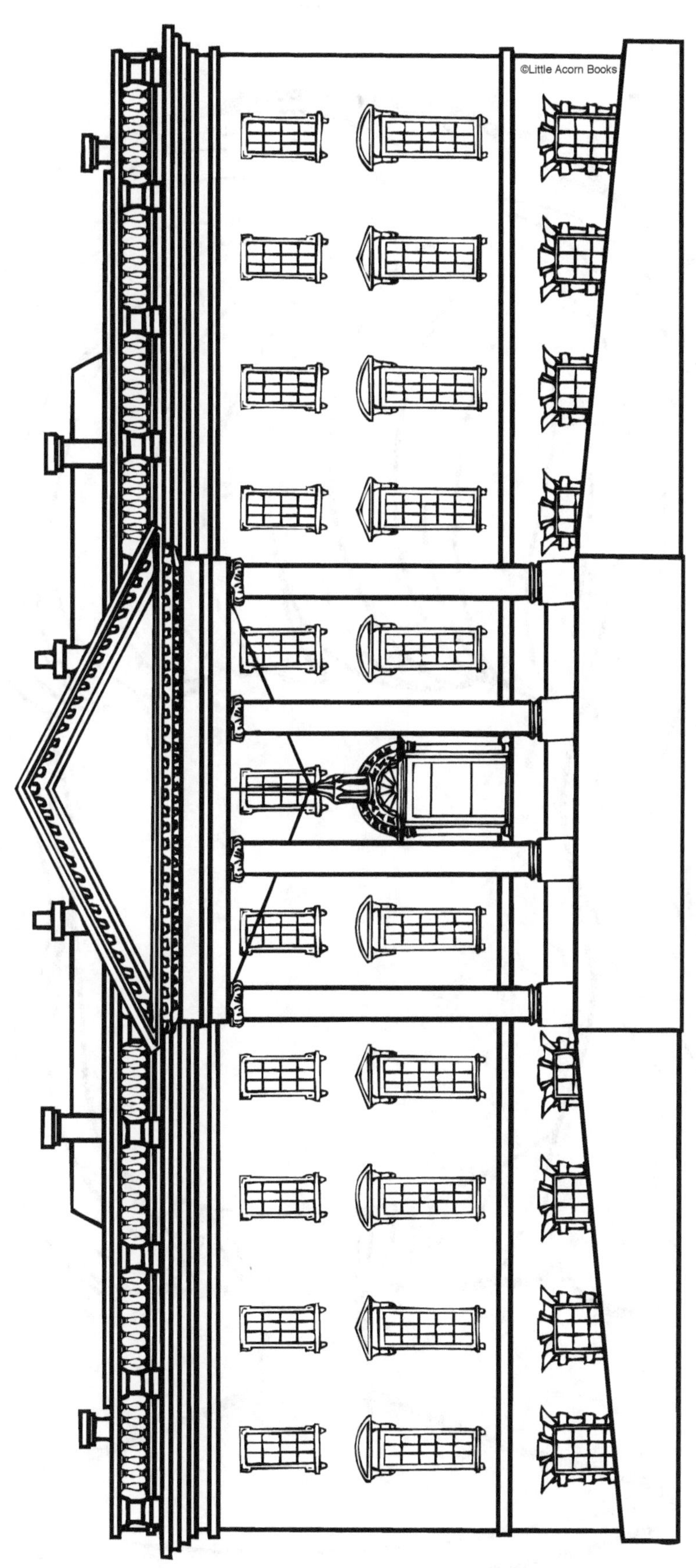

 TPL

wig

 LAB201412P • THE PATTERN LIBRARY • VOLUME TWO • I-Z • 978-1-937257-63-7 • © 2014 Little Acorn Books™

window

Wisconsin, USA

Maps are representations and boundaries are not exact.

wolf (running)

wolf (standing)

wood (cut logs)

wreath (detailed)

LAB201412P • THE PATTERN LIBRARY • VOLUME TWO • I-Z • 978-1-937257-63-7 • © 2014 Little Acorn Books™

wreath (plain)

Wyoming, USA

Maps are representations and boundaries are not exact.

x-ray

xantusia

letter Xx

xylophone

yak

yarn ball

yawn

yo-yo

LAB201412P • THE PATTERN LIBRARY • VOLUME TWO • I-Z • 978-1-937257-63-7 • © 2014 Little Acorn Books™

Yukon, Canada

zebra

zebu

zipper

zither